Date Due

NOV 04 '98			
MAY 27 '00			
Jul 6-3-02			

9/98

Jackson
County
Library
Services

HEADQUARTERS
413 W.Main
Medford, Oregon 97501

Through a Termite City

Carole Telford and

Rod Theodorou

Published by Heinemann Interactive Library,
an imprint of Reed Educational & Professional Publishing Ltd,
1350 East Touhy Avenue, Suite 240 West, Des Plaines, IL 60018

Printed and bound in China

Illustrations by Stephen Ling and Jane Pickering at Linden Artists

Designed by Aricot Vert Design Ltd

02 01 00 99 98

10 9 8 7 6 5 4 3 2 1

Library of Congress Cataloging-in-Publication Data

Theodorou, Rod
    Through a termite city / Rod Theodorou and Carole Telford.
        p.   cm. -- (Amazing journeys)
    Includes bibliographical references and index.
    Summary: Describes the inhabitants, social structure, and activities of an African termite mound.
    ISBN 1-57572-155-4 (lib. bdg.)
    1. Termites--Africa--Juvenile literature.   2. Termites--Nests--Africa--Juvenile literature.   3. Insect societies--Africa--Juvenile literature. [1. Termites.] I. Telford, Carole, 1961-
II. Title. III. Series: Theodorou.
Rod. Amazing journeys.
QL529.26.A1T48 1997
595.7'36--dc21
                                                                        97-13744
                                                                        CIP
                                                                        AC

Some words are shown in bold letters, **like this**. You can find out what these words mean by looking in the Glossary.

Acknowledgments

The author and publishers are grateful to the following for permission to reproduce copyright photographs:

Ardea (Hans D. Dossenbach) pp. 13 (top), 21 (top), 22, (P. Morris) p. 26, (Alan Weaving) p. 12; Bruce Coleman Limited (Gerald Cubitt) p. 6; FLPA p. 11 (top), (Peter Davey) p. 19 (bottom); NHPA (Anthony Bannister) pp. 15, 17 (top), 23 (top and bottom), 27; Oxford Scientific Films (Jen and Des Bartlett) p. 25 (bottom), (Paul Franklin) p. 10, (Sean Morris) p. 13 (bottom), (Ken Oake) p. 17 (bottom), (Alan Root) pp. 11 (bottom), 18, 19 (top), 25 (top), (Kjell Sandved) p. 21 (bottom).

Cover photograph: Oxford Scientific Films

Our thanks to Rob Alcraft for his comments in the preparation of this book.

Every effort has been made to contact copyright holders of any material reproduced in this book. Any omissions will be rectified in subsequent printings if notice is given to the publisher.

Contents

Introduction

You are about to go on an amazing journey. You are going to shrink down smaller than a grain of rice and enter the dark world of an African termite mound. Millions of termites live in this mound, like people in a major city. You will travel through narrow, underground tunnels and watch the termites as they work together to feed and protect their city. You will meet busy workers, and soldiers with huge jaws. You will enter the royal **chamber** and see the king and the swollen, egg-laying queen. As we travel, you will learn how these simple, tiny insects work together to build one of the most amazing nests on earth.

This termite mound belongs to a type of African termite. Up to five million termites may live inside this mound in dark tunnels and chambers.

Termites are insects, about the size of ants. They have much softer bodies than ants, and die if they stay out in the heat of the sun. Even though they are so delicate, there are lots of them. There are about 2000 **species** of termites, living in warm countries all over the world. One reason why they are so successful is that they are one of the few insects that can eat dead plant-matter. There are always plenty of fallen leaves, dry grass, and old tree trunks for the termites to feed on.

They also build nests that are very hard to attack. Different kinds of termites build different kinds of nests. The termites we are going to visit build the tallest, most amazing nests of all.

There are many different species of termites in the world. Most have four castes.

Queen

King

Soldier

Worker

KEY

DISTRIBUTION OF THE TERMITES

Journey Map

Here is the termite mound we are going to travel through. Although the mound looks smooth and solid on the outside, inside it is a **maze** of passages and **chambers**. The huge tower is actually like a tall chimney full of warm air. It keeps the **temperature** just right for the termites. Below the tower is the main termite city, with special areas to store food and feed the young.

Central Chimney

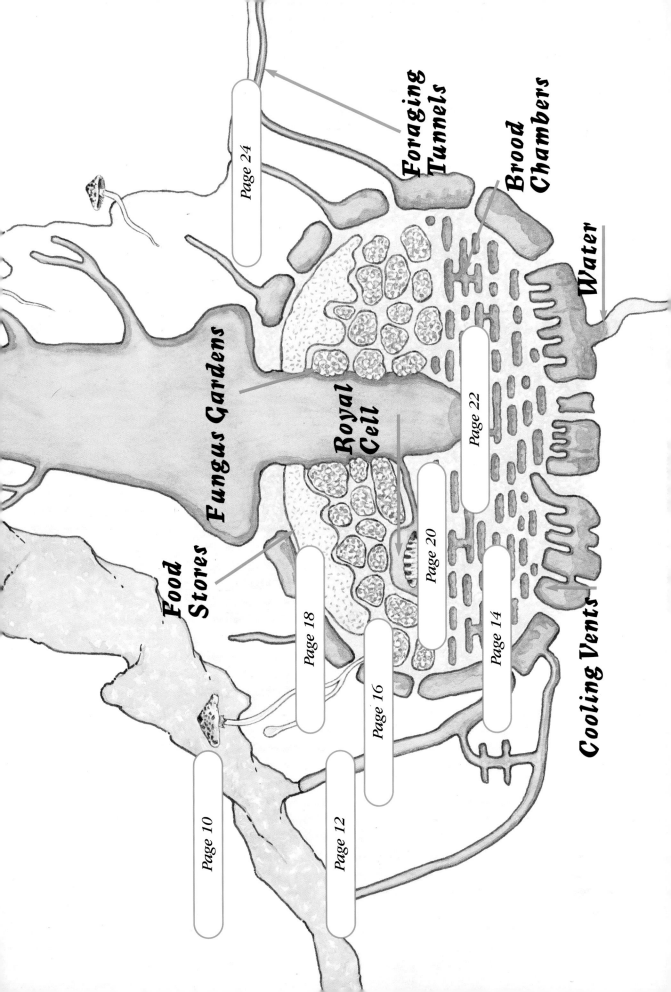

Foraging Tunnels

Brood Chambers

Water

Fungus Gardens

Royal Cell

Food Stores

Cooling Vents

Page 24

Page 22

Page 20

Page 18

Page 16

Page 14

Page 12

Page 10

*W*e are standing in the scorching heat of the African grasslands. We can see a herd of zebra grazing in the distance. A towering shape stands out in front of us. It is a termite mound. Beneath our feet are hidden underground tunnels leading from the mound. Where the tunnels are near the surface, the termites have made tiny, mud-covered paths.

The termites use these paths to go **foraging** for food. We touch the mound. It feels hot, very hard, and lumpy. We can see tiny holes near our feet leading into the mound. It is time to shrink down and see what life is like inside this amazing structure.

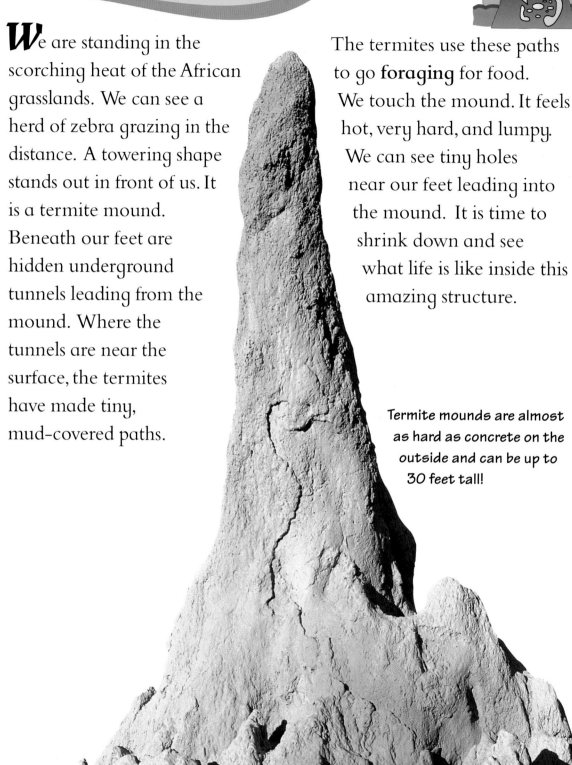

Termite mounds are almost as hard as concrete on the outside and can be up to 30 feet tall!

Dwarf mongoose →

These are often seen sunbathing on termite mounds. From the tall mound, the mongooses can watch out for enemies.

Aardwolf

About the size of a fox, the aardwolf roams the grasslands looking for termites to eat. Instead of attacking the mound, it usually eats termites that are foraging. The aardwolf licks them up.

Assassin bug →

The assassin bug waits outside the mound to kill a worker termite with its spear-like mouth. Then it hides behind the speared, dead worker, sucking it dry, waiting for another termite to kill and eat.

Guardians of the City

We are now less than one-fourth of an inch tall, standing outside one of the entrances to the nest. Above us the **colossal** mound stretches up into the sky. If termites were as big as humans, a termite mound would be a skyscraper five miles high!

Suddenly, three soldier termites appear at the entrance. These guards are always on the alert for intruders. As soon as one soldier senses an enemy nearby, it will pass the message on to other soldiers, who rush to defend the city. One of them is coming toward us, its huge mouthparts raised up to attack. The soldiers are blind and luckily cannot smell us. We move quickly past and enter the dark tunnel.

Termite soldiers will attack anything that tries to enter the mound, even a large animal such as an aardwolf.

Soldiers

The safety of the mound depends on the fighting power of its soldiers. They guard the entrances to the mound and patrol the tunnels inside. Although they are blind, they can detect an intruder by smell and will immediately attack.

Soldiers have big, hard heads with huge muscles to power their massive jaws. Their jaws are so big they cannot feed themselves, so they are fed by the smaller workers.

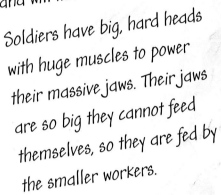

Nasutus soldier

One species of termite has a different kind of soldier. The nasutus soldier has a large spout on its head to squirt sticky poison at an enemy.

Building the Mound

Inside, the mound is like a **maze**. We travel through one dark tunnel after another. They lead off in all directions. The air is warm and moist. We step aside as huge soldiers go by. Some small termites are repairing a tunnel wall. These are worker termites. They are also blind, with white, soft, thin skin and small jaws. They look so weak, and yet these are the termites that built this huge, towering city!

Workers also search for food, feed the soldiers, and look after the king, queen, and eggs. If the mound is attacked, the workers will even join with the soldiers to help fight the enemy.

Most building work takes place in the spring when the rains soften the mud, making it easier for the workers to chew.

Workers

Worker termites build the walls and tunnels by spitting out chewed mud, sand, and plant-matter. When this dries it is very hard. Workers can mend a broken wall or tunnel very quickly.

Termite air conditioning

Termites need to keep air moving through the mound to prevent the tunnels from getting too hot. They build special tunnels, or **vents**, to let cool air into the mound. They even open and close holes to keep the temperature just right.

If the air gets too dry, the termites would quickly die. To keep the air moist inside the mound, the nests are sealed from the outside air.

hot air

hot air

hot air

cool air

cool air

The Fungus Gardens

We move deeper into the mound. It is warmer here and quite damp. This is where the termites grow some of their food. Above us are store **chambers** full of chewed-up leaves and wood, gathered by the workers. In the warm, moist air, this rots like **compost**. A worker takes some of this compost and carries it away to a **honeycomb** of smaller cells. Looking into one of these cells, we see the worker is spreading the compost around just like a good gardener. This is where the termites grow **fungus**. The fungus is fed to those termites that do not leave the city to **forage** for food.

Workers build thin honeycomb gardens, where they grow their fungus food.

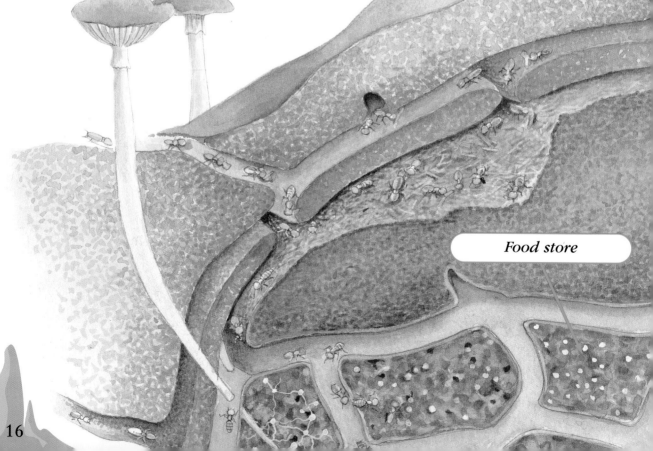

Fungus mushrooms

Food store

Fungus farmers

The type of fungus growing in the termite mound cannot grow anywhere else. Termites and fungus depend on each other for survival.

Mushrooms →

Mushrooms sometimes grow out of the surface of the mound. When these die away, they leave **spores** to grow new fungus. Some scientists think the termites gather up these spores and take them back into the city to grow more fungus.

Gathering food

Blind workers will travel up to 45 yards from the mound looking for dead wood or plants. They travel in underground tunnels, and use scent trails to help them find their way home.

Night Flight

Outside the mound it is night time. It has begun to rain for the first time this year. The workers seem to be excited. They are moving quickly around the tunnels in front of us. Some of them are opening up a tunnel ahead. Suddenly, lots of large termites with long, silvery wings pour through this new opening and scurry past.

This is a special time for the termites. These are the kings and queens of tomorrow. These winged males and females **swarm** out of the holes and fly into the night. Thousands are eaten by **predators**, but some will land and, with luck, they will **mate** and start new nests of their own.

Winged termites leave the mound. After a while, the workers seal up the holes and push some winged termites back to wait for another night.

A new king and queen?

When the winged termites land, they break off their own wings. Each male follows a female until they find a place to dig a hole and start their nest.

Predators →

Many of the winged termites will be killed and eaten on this flight. Large toads also like damp, wet nights. They snatch up as many termites as they can eat.

Lilac-breasted rollers and bats catch termites as they fly. Other hungry predators feast on the termites on the ground.

Into the Royal Cell

The mound is peaceful again. We move downward, following our map carefully. We slide down through a small hole into a large **chamber**. We can hardly believe our eyes. Before us is a mass of workers and soldiers surrounding one massive creature. This is the queen of the city. Her huge, white body is swollen with eggs. Next to her is the large king and scurrying workers who feed and clean her. Every few seconds, we see shiny white eggs being laid. She may lay as many as 30,000 eggs in a day! The workers carry them off to the **brood chambers**.

The queen is 4 inches long and constantly lays eggs.

The queen

The queen termite is more like a prisoner than a ruler. She must spend all her life in the royal cell; she may live to be 50 years old!

The King

The king termite can be seen next to his mate. Like the queen, he is fed by the workers and is too big to squeeze out of the tiny cell doors.

Defending the queen

The royal cell is in the heart of the mound. Only a few narrow passages lead to the cell, and these are protected by soldiers. If the mound is attacked by ants, the royal cell is one of the easiest places to defend.

The Brood Chambers

We leave the royal cell and follow one of the workers who is carrying a newly laid egg. Suddenly, our flashlight catches thousands of white eggs in its beam. It is an amazing sight. Worker termites are hurrying about, acting as nurses for the eggs. Our worker carefully places the egg it is carrying alongside the other eggs.

If we move along further, taking care not to step on any eggs, we can see the baby **nymph** termites as they hatch. A nurse termite gently feeds the nymph. Some nymphs are bigger and more developed than others. After about three months, they are old enough to take their place in the termite colony.

Warm and well fed by the workers, these white nymphs are safe in the brood chamber.

Nymphs

Nymphs are young, adult termites. They have soft, white bodies. They shed their skin several times as they grow.

Workers or soldiers?

Workers feed the nymphs special food. The nymphs can grow into workers or soldiers, depending on the kind of food they are given. If the city needs more soldiers, the workers will feed them only soldier food. In this way, the colony has the right number of termites for the work they need.

Under Attack!

Suddenly, the whole mound is shaking. The tunnel we are in is crumbling! The mound is under attack! Termites all around us are running along tunnels. Some nurse termites push past carrying eggs.

They are moving them to a safer part of the mound. Soldiers rush toward the noise and shaking of the attack. There is an escape tunnel just in front of us. It leads us right outside the mound. We run through an opening into the cool night air. It is dark, but it is easy to see what the attacker is. A massive animal is digging a hole in the city walls with its huge claws. It is time to end our journey and return to our normal size!

Aardvarks do damage termite mounds, but they do not destroy them. The termites always repair the mound, which can last for 60 years!

Aardvark

The aardvark looks rather like a pig with long, floppy ears. Aardvarks have strong legs and long claws for digging into mounds so they can lick up the termites. They also dig burrows in the ground to hide from enemies.

Pangolin ⟶

Like the aardvark, the pangolin will also dig into termite mounds. It is covered in sharp scales and has a long, thin, sticky tongue to lick up termites. To protect it from the bites of soldier termites, it has thick eyelids and can close its nostrils.

Ant attack

Driver ants are the termites' worst enemy. They sometimes attack the mound by the thousands, ripping open the walls and fighting terrible battles deep inside the mound with the smaller soldier termites. Then they carry away the dead termites to eat them.

Termites and People

Hungry termites can cause terrible problems for people. They can eat crops such as sugar canes, potatoes, or yams. They can also attack wooden houses. Sometimes, no damage can be seen on the outside, while the termites are busy eating away the inside of timbers and beams. With a sudden crash, the whole house collapses!

Termites will also attack things inside houses, such as leather clothes, rubber, wooden furniture, and even books! One village in India had to be abandoned because of termite damage. In many parts of the world, wooden houses are now sprayed with **chemicals** that stop the termites from attacking the wood.

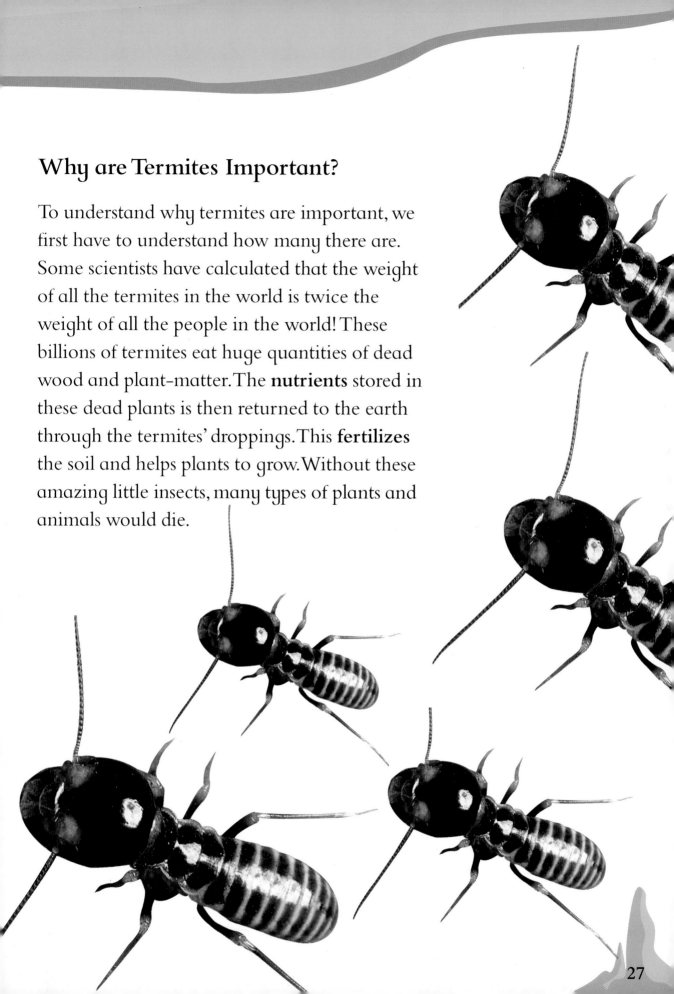

Why are Termites Important?

To understand why termites are important, we first have to understand how many there are. Some scientists have calculated that the weight of all the termites in the world is twice the weight of all the people in the world! These billions of termites eat huge quantities of dead wood and plant-matter. The **nutrients** stored in these dead plants is then returned to the earth through the termites' droppings. This **fertilizes** the soil and helps plants to grow. Without these amazing little insects, many types of plants and animals would die.

Glossary

brood chambers	These are places where young termites are fed and looked after.
caste	These are different groups.
chamber	This is an enclosed space or room.
chemicals	These are liquids and sprays that have strong effects.
colossal	This means enormous.
compost	This is a mixture of rotting plants that makes the soil richer and that helps plants grow.
fertilize	This means to make the soil richer.
forage	This means to look for food.
fungus	This is a simple plant, like a mushroom.
honeycomb	This is a maze of chambers joined to each other.
lilac-breasted roller	This is a bird that catches flying termites.
mate	This means when a male animal and a female animal get together to reproduce.
maze	This is a complicated network of passages.
nutrients	These are parts of food that makes living things healthy.
nymph	This is a young, adult termite.
predators	These are animals that hunt and kill other animals for food.

species	This is a group of living things that are very similar.
spores	These are seedlike cells that are produced by fungi, and that grow into new fungi.
swarm	This is a large number of termites joining together in flight.
temperature	This is how hot or cold something is.
vents	These are holes that allow fresh air in.

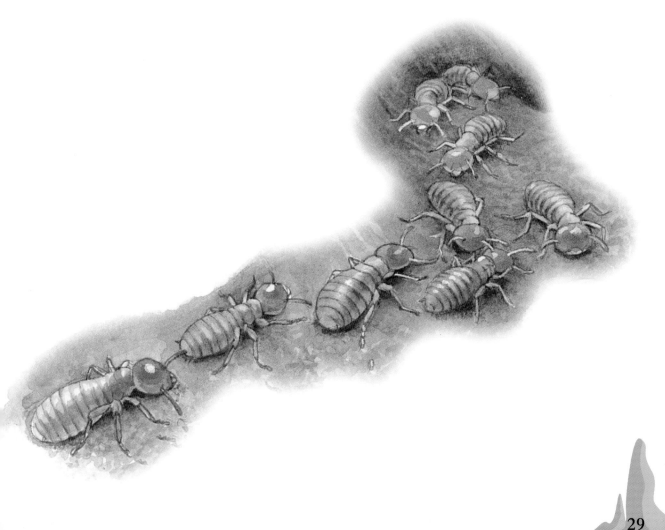

More Books to Read

Armstrong, Bev. *Insects*. Santa Barbara, Cal: Learning Works, 1990.

Bailes, Edith G. *But Will It Bite Me?* A Reference Book of Insects for Children & Their Grownups. Richmond, Me: Cardamom, 1985.

Berger, Melvin. *Insect Lives*. New York: Newbridge Communications, 1995.

Brandt, Keith. *Insects*. Mahwah, N.J.: Troll Communications, 1985.

George, Michael. *Insects*. Plymouth, Minn: Childs World, 1991.

Goor, Ron & Nancy. *Metamorphosis: From Egg to Adult*. New York: Atheneum, 1990.

Hunt, Joni P. *Insects*. New York: Dorling Kindersley, 1990.

Johnson, Jinny. *Bugs: A Closer Look at the World's Tiny Creatures*. New York: Readers Digest Kids, 1995.

Kirkpatrick, Rena K. *Look at Insects*. Austin, Tex: Raintree Steck-Vaughn, 1985.

Lampton, Christopher. *Insect Attack*. Brookfield, Conn: Millbrook Press, 1992.

Oda, Hidetomo. *Insects & Homes*. Austin, Tex: Raintree Steck-Vaughn, 1986.

Other Resources

Audio Recordings
Chapin, Tom. Mother Earth. A & M Records.

Raffi. Evergreen, Everblue. Troubadour Records.

Rogers, Sally. Piggyback Planet: Songs for a Whole Earth. Round River Records.

Video Recordings
Understanding Ecology Series: What is a Food Chain? Coronet © 1992. VHS, 11 minutes. (Also available on videodisk.)

Understanding Ecology Series: What is a Habitat? Coronet © 1991. VHS, 13 minutes. (Also available on videodisk.)

Understanding Ecology Series: What is an Ecosystem? Coronet © 1992. VHS, 11 minutes. (Also available on videodisk.)

Organizations

The Cousteau Society
70 Greenbrier Circle, Suite 402
Chesapeake, VA 23320
Tel (757) 523-9335

Greenpeace
1436 U Street NW
Washington, D.C. 20009
Tel. (202) 462-1177

National Wildlife Federation
8925 Leesburg Pike
Vienna, VA 22184
Tel (703) 790-4100

Nature Conservancy
International Headquarters
1815 North Lynn Street
Arlington, Virginia 22209
Tel (703) 841-5300

River Watch Network
153 State Street
Montpelier, VT 05602
Tel (802) 223-3840

Sierra Club
85 Second Street, Second Floor
San Francisco, CA 94105-3441
Tel 415-977-5500

Index